YOUR BODY BATTLES A STOMACHACHE

WRITTEN BY **VICKI COBB**   PHOTOMICROGRAPHS BY **DENNIS KUNKEL**
ILLUSTRATIONS BY **ANDREW N. HARRIS**

Ⓜ Millbrook Press / Minneapolis

NOTE: The photomicrographs in this book were taken with a scanning electron microscope (SEM). The photos are originally in black and white. A computer program is used to add color, often to highlight interesting features. The colors used do not show the real colors of the subject. The × followed by a number indicates magnification. For example, ×250 means the object in the picture is 250 times larger than its real size.

The author gratefully acknowledges David O Matson, M.D., PhD. Professor of Health Professions and Pediatrics, Graduate Program in Public Health, Eastern Virginia Medical School, Norfolk, VA; and thanks Mary Slamin and Gail Fell, children's librarians from the Greenburgh Public Library.

For Jillian Davis Cobb —VC

This series is dedicated to my mom, Carmen Kunkel, for the care she gives her children and grandchildren —DK

For Mom, who always made me feel better —ANH

Text copyright © 2009 by Vicki Cobb
Photomicrographs © 2009 by Dennis Kunkel
Illustrations copyright © 2009 by Lerner Publishing Group, Inc.

3 6830 00101 4818

Additional photographs in this book are reproduced with the permission of: © David M. Martin, M.D./Photo Researchers, Inc., pp. 11, 15.

Millbrook Press
A division of Lerner Publishing Group, Inc.
241 First Avenue North
Minneapolis, MN 55401 U.S.A.

Website address: www.lernerbooks.com

Library of Congress Cataloging-in-Publication Data

Cobb, Vicki.
    Your body battles a stomachache / by Vicki Cobb ; with photomicrographs by Dennis Kunkel ; illustrations by Andrew N. Harris.
        p. cm. — (Body Battles)
    Includes bibliographical references and index.
    ISBN 978-0-8225-7166-7 (lib. bdg. : alk. paper)
    1. Stomach—Diseases—Juvenile literature. 2. Intestines—Microbiology—Juvenile literature. I. Harris, Andrew, 1977–
ill. II. Title.
RC817.C66 2009
616.3'3—dc22   2008002852

Manufactured in the United States of America
1 2 3 4 5 6 – DP – 14 13 12 11 10 09

Don't you just hate to get a stomachache? Your tummy hurts. You throw up. You run to the toilet because you have diarrhea. The whole thing is no fun. No doubt about it! You've caught a "bug." Think of it as a "cold" that attacks your digestive system. It is like a small war going on in your body—a war you will win because you have teams of superhero cells living inside your body. This is the story of how it all works.

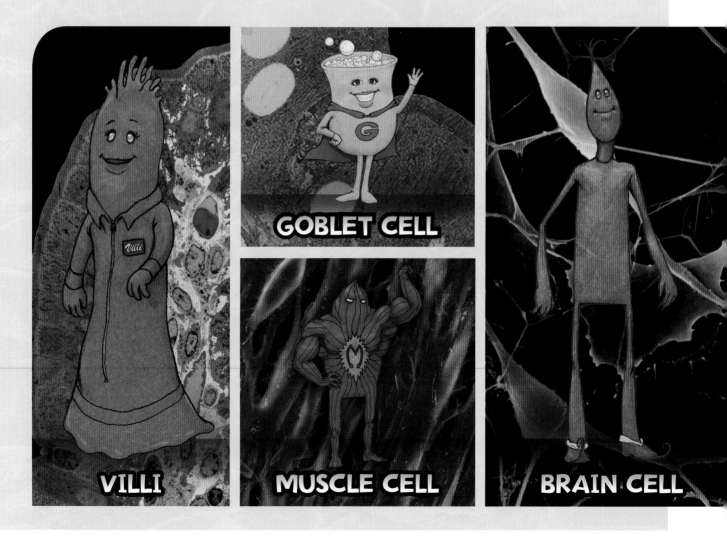

VILLI

GOBLET CELL

MUSCLE CELL

BRAIN CELL

3

The story begins with what you eat. Your whole body, including your mouth and stomach, is made of very tiny living things called cells. All living things are made of cells, including the food you eat.

x325

x225

x80

x665

4

Cells are so tiny that they can only be seen with a microscope—a very powerful magnifying glass. Different cells do different jobs. Muscle cells let you move. Nerve cells tell muscle cells to move and allow you to sense the world. Blood cells carry oxygen to all cells. And bone cells make bone and keep it strong.

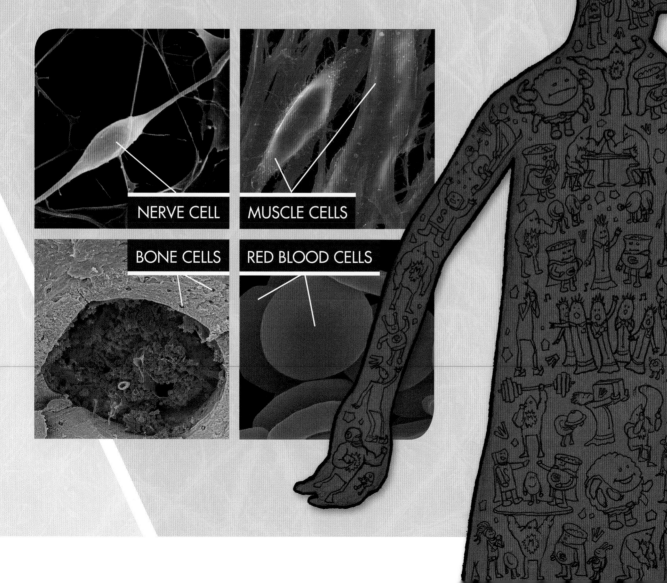

NERVE CELL

MUSCLE CELLS

BONE CELLS

RED BLOOD CELLS

What, then, are cells made of? Something extremely small! The building blocks of cells are called molecules. They are so small that they cannot be seen with even the strongest microscope.

FAT

PROTEIN

CARBOHYDRATES

Every cell is made from millions of molecules. Three kinds of molecules are found in all cells. They are fats, proteins, and carbohydrates. If these names sound like words connected with food, you are right. Molecules in celery cells are arranged differently from steak cells or your brain cells. But each kind of cell contains some of the same molecules.

When you digest food, your body breaks it down into molecules. Chewing food and mixing it with saliva is the beginning of digestion. Saliva starts working on starches, a form of carbohydrate. See for yourself. Chew a plain soda cracker (a starch) and hold it in your mouth until it starts tasting sweet. Starches, which don't taste sweet, are actually long chains of small sugar molecules. Saliva breaks up the starch chains into sugars, which taste sweet.

While the saliva is starting to work on starches, your chewed food becomes a round ball you can swallow. This ball is called a bolus. When you swallow you send the bolus through a 10-inch-long tube called the esophagus. The bolus doesn't just fall into the stomach. The muscles of the esophagus squeeze together right above the bolus, pushing it down into the stomach. This squeezing is called peristalsis. Peristalsis squeezes the bolus the way you squeeze toothpaste to push it out of the tube.

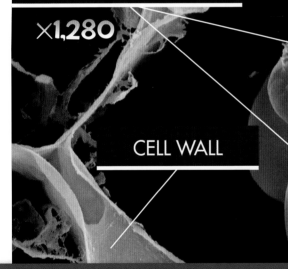

POTATO STARCH GRAINS

×1,280

CELL WALL

This photomicrograph shows starch grains inside the cell of a potato. You can see the wall of the cell surrounding the grains.

Digestion of proteins and fats breaks up these large molecules into smaller ones that can go into the blood. Your cells use these food molecules to build new cells and repair old cells. They also give you energy.

The bolus enters the stomach. Your stomach is a muscular bag. It is about as big as your hand when your thumb is touching the tips of your pointer and middle finger. Your stomach can stretch if you eat a big meal. Your stomach's job is to mix the chewed food with strong juices. It churns them together like a food processor would until much of the food is broken down into molecules.

MIX

CHURN

DIGEST

Small Intestine

A very strong chemical, an acid, is added in the stomach to digest proteins. (This acid is what gives vomit its sour taste.) After four hours, all the food becomes a liquid. It leaves the stomach to go into your intestines.

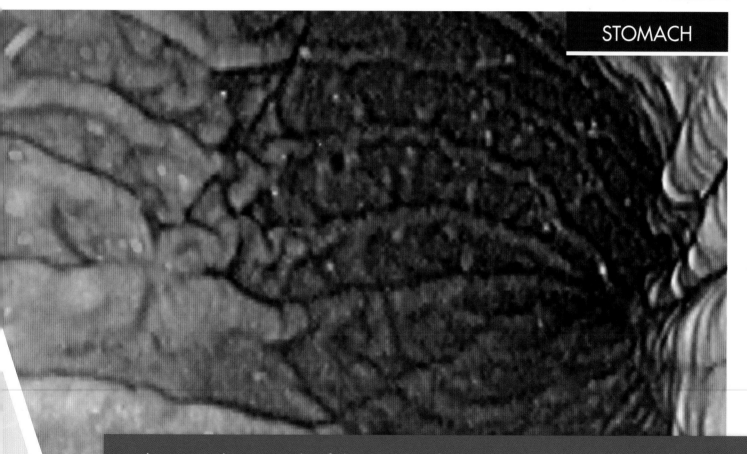

STOMACH

This is a photograph of the inside of a stomach taken with a special camera called a gastroscope. It shows mucus-coated folds of a stomach. The folds allow the stomach to expand as it fills with food.

Your intestines are also called your guts. There are two kinds of intestines: small and large. The small intestines are a narrow tube. This tube is about 16 feet (5 meters) long. It is folded back and forth on itself so that it can fit into your abdomen.

Inside, the small intestine is lined with tiny fingerlike extensions called villi. They absorb molecules of digested food into your blood. Villi have an extremely thin skin that molecules can pass through. Inside the villi are tiny tubes carrying blood. The blood picks up the food molecules and moves them to every single cell in your body. Your cells use food molecules to build new cells and repair old cells. Food molecules also give you energy.

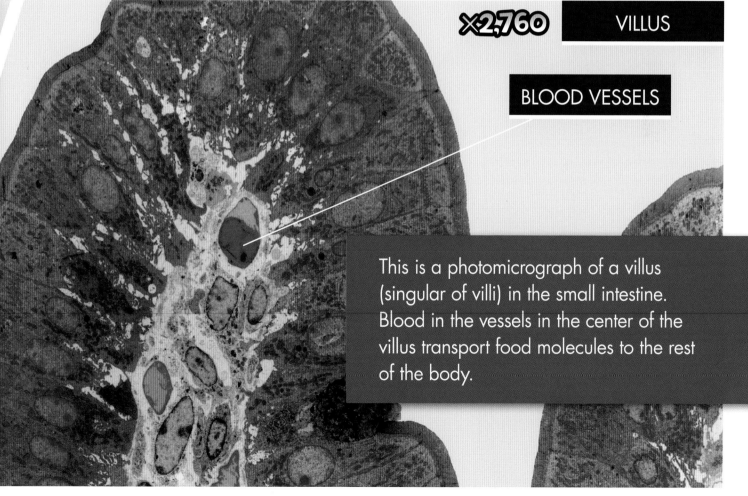

X2,760   VILLUS

BLOOD VESSELS

This is a photomicrograph of a villus (singular of villi) in the small intestine. Blood in the vessels in the center of the villus transport food molecules to the rest of the body.

Not all the material in your small intestines is absorbed. The material that isn't absorbed passes through to your large intestine. The large intestine is a shorter, fatter tube that runs up, across, and down around your small intestines. Its main job is to remove water and salt from the undigested food, which is very watery when it enters the large intestine. After the water is absorbed, the undigested food that's left leaves your body when you move your bowels.

ESOPHAGUS

STOMACH

LARGE INTESTINE

SMALL INTESTINE

When you get a stomachache, normal digestion is interrupted.

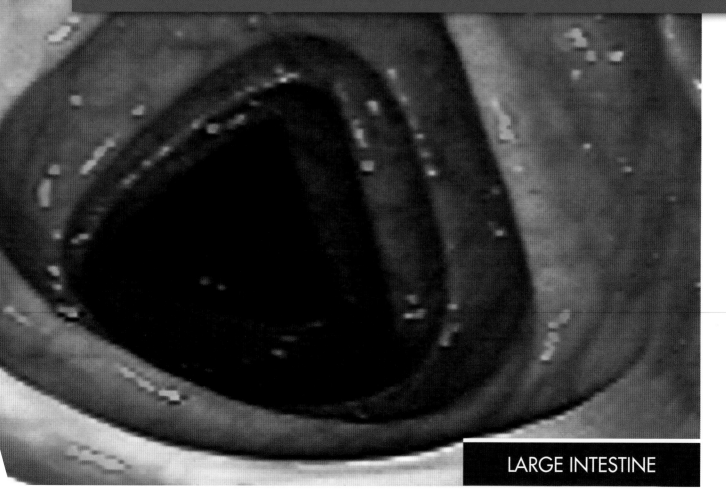

By the time the material in the small intestines reaches the large intestine, most of the water and nutrients have been absorbed. So the large intestine needs strong muscles to move along the waste material. Here the intestine is empty, so you can see the powerful triangular-shape muscles.

LARGE INTESTINE

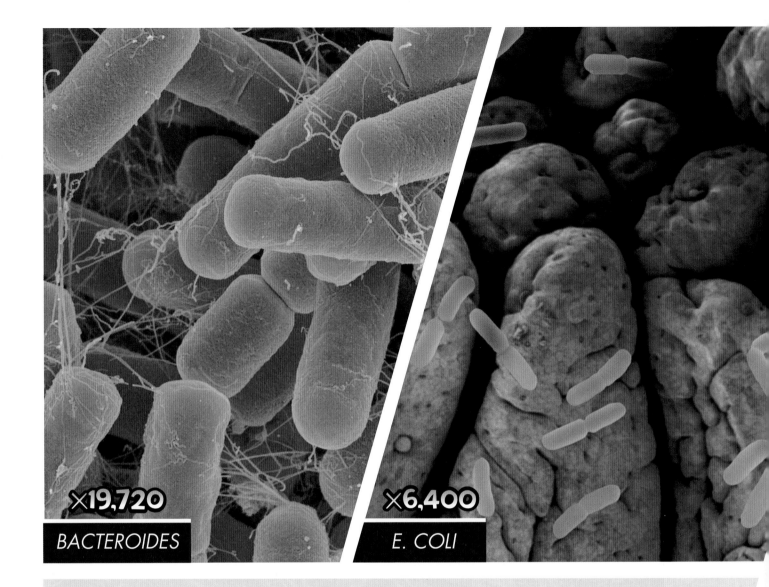

×19,720

BACTEROIDES

×6,400

E. COLI

Some stomachaches are caused by bacteria. Not all bacteria are bad, though. *Bacteroides* is one of the most common of at least 30 or 40 different kinds of good bacteria. These good bacteria are constantly growing in your intestines. They make up more than half the weight of your feces! But harmful bacteria, such as *E. coli,* can cause stomachaches.

In rare cases, parasites such as *Giardia* or tapeworm can also cause stomachaches. The most common kinds of stomachaches, however, are caused by a virus.

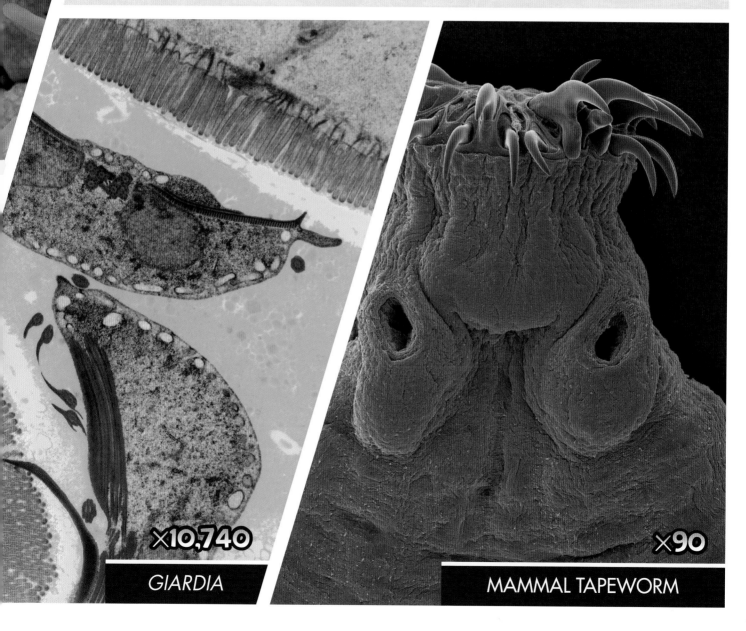

×10,740

GIARDIA

×90

MAMMAL TAPEWORM

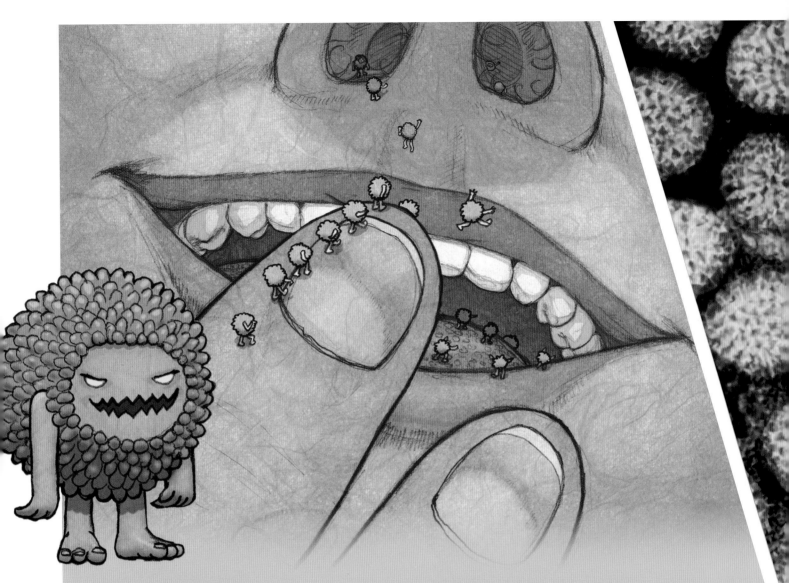

A stomachache can start when a virus enters your body, perhaps from dirty hands. A virus is a very small germ, smaller than most cells. About half of all stomachaches are caused by viruses. A common example is the rotavirus, which is often the cause of stomachaches in very young children. It got its name because *rota* means "wheel-like."

A rotavirus has to attack other cells in order to reproduce itself. It is much smaller than your body's cells. It looks like a 20-sided soccer ball with lots of tiny spots on it.

×795,400

ROTAVIRUS

A rotavirus attaches itself to a cell in the villi of the small intestine. Then it uses the parts of your villi cell that it needs to copy itself. It's like your cell is a factory and the virus steals its machinery to manufacture itself. In the process, it kills your cell and releases the newly made viruses to attack other cells.

GERMCO

21

When new rotaviruses burst out of the cells making up the villi, the villi cells die. But your body doesn't take this attack lying down! Fluids rush into the small intestine through openings left by the injured cells. A lot of the fluid is mucus. Goblet cells in the walls of the intestine make mucus. They are the same cells that make mucus in your nose. Mucus lubricates the flow in the intestine. When you get sick, extra mucus helps wash the germs from your body, just like your nose runs when you have a cold.

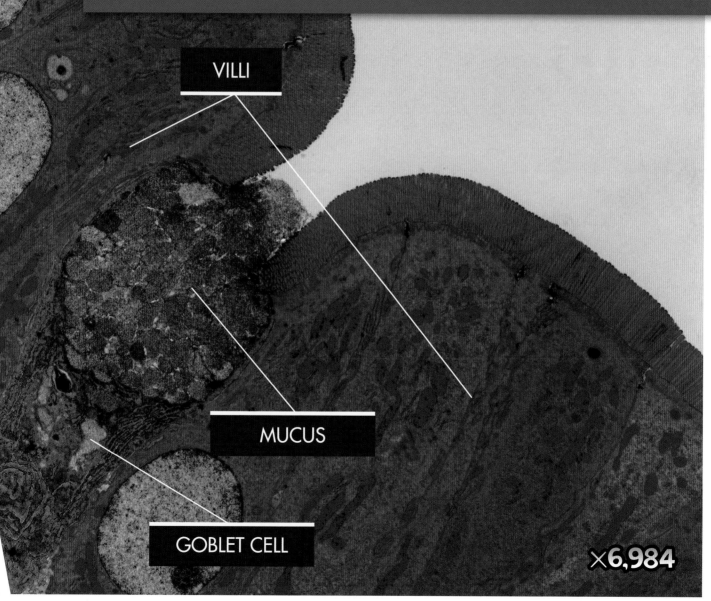

Goblet cells live in the wall of the intestine. They make mucus to lubricate the flow of food. They are like the goblet cells in your nose. When you get sick, the goblet cells make a lot more mucus very quickly.

VILLI

MUCUS

GOBLET CELL

×6,984

The injured cells give off a juice that makes nerve cells send a pain message to your brain. The pain gets your attention so that you start taking care of yourself. The injured cells also send a message to a center in your brain that can make you throw up. The brain sends out a message so that you squeeze the muscles just below your ribs. Then these muscles relax while your esophagus does a reverse peristalsis.

The smell of vomit comes from some of the digestive juices that work on your food in the beginning of the small intestine.

These movements are called retching. After a few retching cycles, the contents of your stomach come out of your mouth.

When you're sick, fluid pours into the small intestines to help wash away the viruses. Your intestines are not able to absorb all the extra liquid, so you get diarrhea.

Your body can lose a lot of fluid when you are sick. And your cells need fluid. That's why it's important to drink a lot of water when you have diarrhea.

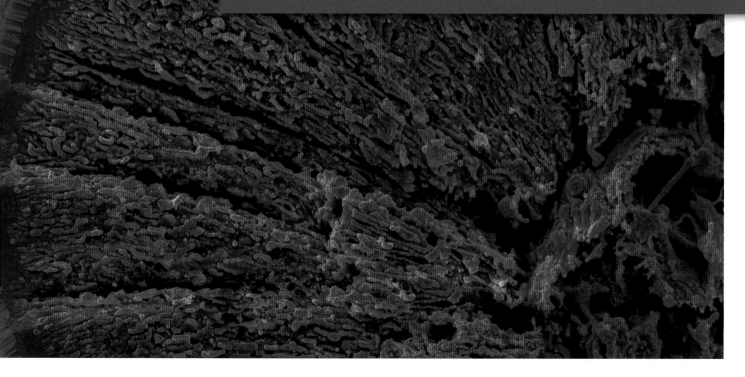

×3,750   **VILLI CROSS SECTION**

This is a slice through a villus of the small intestine. Healthy villi absorb fluid in your intestines. When rotaviruses attack your body, the villi can't absorb all the fluid your body makes.

After a day or two, you'll start to feel better. Your intestines are repairing themselves. The injured villi are banding together to stop the flow of extra mucus and fluids from damaged cells. After about a week, the repairs are complete. New cells have replaced the ones that have died. Your intestines are back in business.

Once again, the small intestine absorbs food molecules and your large intestine absorbs liquid. Your appetite returns and food tastes good again. Another amazing job turned in by the cells of your body! What a relief!

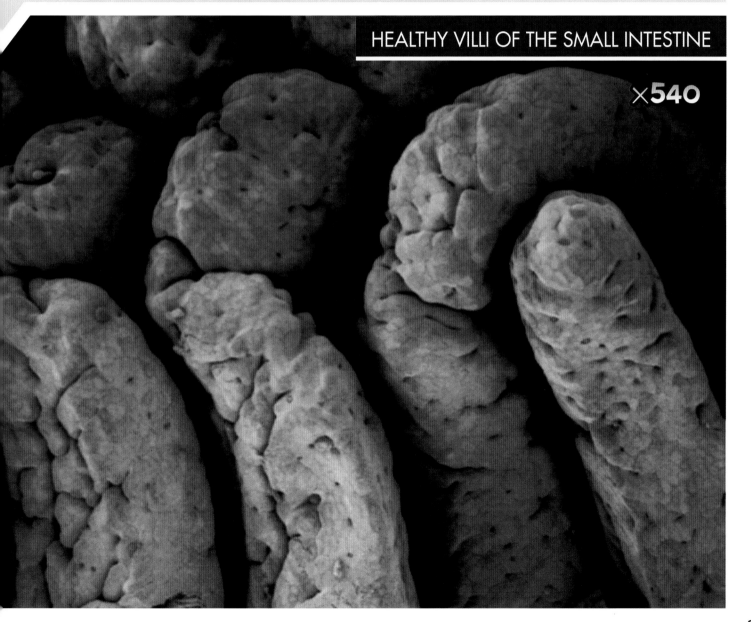

HEALTHY VILLI OF THE SMALL INTESTINE

×540

GLOSSARY

acid: a watery, sour liquid that reacts with other substances. Stomach acid helps digest food.

bolus: a ball-shaped mass of chewed food and saliva

carbohydrate: compound such as sugar and starch that contains molecules made of carbon, hydrogen, and oxygen

cell: the smallest unit of all living things considered to be alive. The smallest living things have only one cell. Human beings are multicelled.

diarrhea: watery or loose bowel movements

digestion: the process by which food is reduced to its molecules so that it can be absorbed into the bloodstream. The organs that do this are called the digestive tract.

esophagus: the muscular tube that connects the back of the throat to the stomach

fats: one of the three main classes of food that are a source of energy for the body

intestines: the long, tubelike organ that finishes the digestion of food

large intestine: the last part of the digestive tract that connects the small intestine to the rectum. The large intestine absorbs water from the food remains that are not absorbed into the body.

molecule: the smallest particle of a substance that has all the properties of the substance. Molecules are made of atoms.

peristalsis: wavelike contractions of the esophagus and intestines to move food along through the digestive tract

photomicrograph: a photograph taken through a microscope

proteins: one of the three main classes of food and a source of building materials for the body

rotavirus: the most common kind of virus to cause a stomachache. It attacks the beginning of the small intestine.

small intestine: the part of the digestive tract between the stomach and the large intestine. It is about 20 feet long (6 m) in the average adult. Its job is to absorb food molecules into the bloodstream.

starches: large carbohydrates made up of chains of sugar molecules. In digestion, starches are broken down into sugars, which are absorbed into the blood.

stomach: a bean-shaped, baglike organ that connects the base of the esophagus to the beginning of the small intestine. It breaks down large food molecules into smaller ones so that they can be absorbed into the blood.

villi (singular villus): fingerlike projections of the inside of the small intestine that increase its surface area, allowing it to absorb more food molecules into the blood

virus: a very small microorganism that cannot reproduce unless it invades another living cell

FURTHER READING

Corcoran, Mary K. *The Quest to Digest.* Watertown, MA: Charlesbridge, 2006.

Gold, Susan Dudley. *The Digestive and Excretory Systems.* Berkeley Heights, NJ: Enslow, 2004.

Houghton, Gillian. *Guts: The Digestive System.* New York: PowerKids Press, 2007.

Johnson, Rebecca L. *The Digestive System.* Minneapolis: Lerner Publications Company, 2005.

Royston, Angela. *Why Do I Vomit: And Other Questions about Digestion.* Chicago: Heinemann, 2002.

Simon, Seymour. *Guts: Our Digestive System.* New York: HarperCollins, 2005.

WEBSITES

Discovery Kids

http://yucky.discovery.com/flash/body/pg000126.html
Easy to digest discussion of how the digestive system works

http://yucky.discovery.com/flash/body/yuckystuff/vomit/js.index.html
A description of what happens when you vomit—with lots of cool facts

Kids Health

http://kidshealth.org/kid/stay_healthy/body/bowel.html
A good description of what goes on in the body when you have diarrhea

http://kidshealth.org/kid/ill_injure/sick/stomach_flu.html
Information for kids on what happens when you get stomach flu

Nemours Foundation

http://www.kidshealth.org/kid/body/digest_noSW.html
Learn how your body breaks down the food you eat.

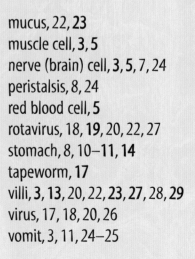

INDEX